THE

SECRET

TO

CAREER

HAPPINESS

A Manual to
Loving What You Do,
Earning More Than You Need,
And Doing the World Good

By

James Lopata

From the creator of the popular Career
innerOvation *program, with work published in*
The New York Times *and* Boston Globe *and*
heard on National Public Radio

with Brenda Loan Baker

First Printing: June 16, 2016

innerOvation LLC
1 Broadway, 14th Floor,
Cambridge, MA 02142
www.innerOvation.com

ISBN: 1533398925

ISBN-13: 978-1533398925

DEDICATION

To everyone who desires a happy, full, rich, meaningful life.

.

CONTENTS

ACKNOWLEDGMENTS

Thank you especially to Brenda Loan Baker, without whom, this book would not exist. Thanks also to my other business partners George Loan Baker and Alicia Davis, and to my parents Casey and Mary Ellen Lopata; to my amazing coach Harry Faddis; to the incomparable Jonathan (Jeb) Bates, owner of the amazing Results System™ ,who has inspired, supported, and helped me beyond measure, and so many others, including: Tom Concannon, Judy Ozbun, Jonathan, Lavash, Jack Vendetti, Jim Smith, DJ Hallett, Brian Ganson, John Todd, Jim Voltz, Chris Rebera, Mitch Finnegan, Stan Lopata, my entire family, Imtiyaz Hussein, and all the members of my book discussion group, Dan Cosio, John Bethard, Chris Nix, Neil Eisenberg, Dustin Dietrich, Shauna Gullbrand, Robert Dimmick, Malia Lazu, Justin Richardson, Ryan Tyler Smith, Randy Bock, Janice Hart, Marc LaCasse, Glen Kewley, John Basile, David Brown, Jamie Crisman, Stephanie Marisca, Sherry Dutra, and the iPEC coaching community, Rob Haslam, Eric Santamaria, Steve Martin, Jorge Bonilla, Benoit Denizet-Lewis, Michael Kuchwara, Sydney Rice, Marilyn Humphries, Alex Walling, Kathy Poehnert, Alan Cohen, Jim Arnoff, Paul Twitchell, Audrey Holst, Mark Eron, Marty Carey, Eliott Goodwin, James Ashton, Trishia Lichauco, Pam Cuming, Mike Conway, John Stasio, Wil Fisher, Sydney Janey, Anne Sasser, Betsy Cowan, Keith Hunt, Elizabeth Hoenscheid, T. Michael Thomas, Dan Hochman, Pam Garramone, Randy Bock, Kirk Haddon, Daniel Schreiner, Chris Clough, Alex Harper, Peter Zimmer, Art Nava, Cam Adibi, Sarah Ginand, Kate Houlihan, Kevin Cann, Nathan Irizarry, Stan Dutton, Audrey Rapoport, Jonathan Liebman, all my amazing clients, and David Zimmerman, Rob Phelps, Dean Burchell, Loren King, Scott Kearnan, and countless others (please forgive me if I forgot you!), who have supported me, believed in me, heard me go on and on and on about writing and publishing a book (finally, right?!) and helped me to shape and share this content in an effort to make everyone happy in what they do, and, consequently, to make the world a happier, better place. Thank you!!!
— *James Lopata.*

1

GETTING STARTED

Nine out of ten workers express high levels of dissatisfaction in their work lives.

That's a pretty astounding figure when you think about it. It's awfully sad too.

Are you one of them? I was. And so was my co-author, Brenda.

These workers find themselves watching the clock at best. Or overwhelmed and frustrated. Or, at worst, maybe even a little homicidal!

The statistics get even more depressing when you learn that fewer than one percent actually REALLY love what they spend nearly half of their waking hours engaged in!

I know this from working with a lot of dissatisfied professionals.

Why are so many people unhappy with their careers? What does it take to become one of the happy ones?

In this book, Brenda and I will share reasons why so many find themselves grinding away for hours, days, months, and years, and live lives that are deeply dissatisfying. More importantly, we will share our approach for getting out of the career death trap—all the elements you need to end up in the one percent of happy workers.

We've employed this process to great success with countless individuals and in groups and classes. We've even quantified it. Many folks who have rated their job satisfaction level at a 2 on a scale of 10 (as the happiest) have gone to jobs they rate as 10 or even, 11 out of 10! (Some of them are quite enthusiastic about the results!) And we've done this with all kinds of workers: across all genders and experience levels—millennials, baby-boomers, those just embarking on work life, and mid-lifers seeking change. And we've helped professionals of all stripes: Fortune 500 executives, CEOs, Hollywood entertainers, startup entrepreneurs, healthcare professionals, food service workers, retail clerks, Wall Street bankers, small business owners, middle managers, creative designers, government employees, and more.

They found work they truly love that pays them more than they need and provides meaning in their lives.

Sound too good to be true?

Check out a few examples:

One professional initially rated his job happiness at 2 on a scale of 10. In fact, he didn't believe any people actually loved their jobs at all. Yowza! I am pleased to report that he now works for a company where employees all rate 10 or 11 on the job happiness scale.

Another person spent 9 years in a job, 7 of them hating it, stuck. He worried the golden handcuffs were going to keep him from ever finding employment satisfaction. Within a week after starting this method he got a hot job lead. Four months later he was in a position he absolutely loved—with a 50 percent salary increase!

Another professional took a modest salary cut to find the job of his dreams. He loved his new work so much more that he wasn't spending money, needlessly trying to make himself happy outside of his work. His net worth has gone up. And he enjoys himself a lot more.

How did they do it? Not the way most people do it—the way that often lands them in job hell.

They took the path outlined in this book, which I stumbled on through my own trial and error building my own career path.

A New Career Path

I grew up at the end of an era when people could expect to get a job with a big corporation, move up the ranks, get promotions and salary increases and retire comfortably. Most of my classmates tried that path. They got downsized, frustrated and unhappy all along life's journey. I took a different path. I don't know why, but I did. And it's made all the difference, not just to me, but to countless others I have helped. Consider what I've done in my life:

I'm a Grammy voter from my work in the music business. I appeared in a Hollywood film with Mira Sorvino. I sang at Carnegie Hall. I've worked as a Vice President on Wall Street, creating some of the finance industry's first web and online presences while working with staff in Asia, and Europe. As a writer and commentator, I have been heard on National Public Radio. I have been published in the Boston Globe and the New York Times. I sang at actress Isabella Rossellini's children's baptism. I have been an Internet consultant, working with clients in France.

Mid-career, I acquired a master's degree from Harvard in theology. I have become a spiritual advisor and a teacher of meditation and mind-training techniques. I now work at the Cambridge Innovation Center near MIT where I coach and consult game-changing C-level business professionals and leaders, and small business owners and startups. I have absolutely loved what I've done through the years. I've made money and made a difference in the world. And I've had a blast doing it! Now I love helping people find careers they love.

So what did I do different than everyone else? What did I do that has brought happiness to my life? What secrets did I discover that I now share with others to help them move from 2-rated jobs to 10-rated jobs they love?

The Biggest Job Search Mistake

The main thing I discovered was that most people go about career development in the wrong way. As kids, we spend a lot of time trying to decide what we want to BE when I grow up. That's the right question. But when it comes to actually getting a job, we spend most of our time trying to figure out what we want to DO. Being and doing are two very different things.

We are human beings, not human doings.

When we focus on what we want to do rather than on who we want to be, we set ourselves up for disaster.

The biggest problem that lands people in miserable jobs is that they look for a job to begin with.

But how can you find a job if you're not looking for one?

I know, that doesn't sound like it makes sense. Stay with me.

Here are two of the biggest problems with looking for a job.

First, consider that only 20% of available jobs are ever posted or advertised. That means you are not going to know about 80% of available jobs if you're just looking on Google searches.

Even worse. When you're scouring monster dot com or LinkedIn, or reading job descriptions, what are you doing? You're looking for a job somebody else has defined. It's like you read a job description and you automatically begin to think "how can I fit into that"? It's like walking around looking at holes in a wall and trying to figure out how you are going to whittle yourself to fit into them. Get out a knife and start peeling yourself down.

OUCH!

That's why we are miserable in our jobs. Got it? Don't try to find a job someone else has defined. Don't! It's a recipe for disaster!

"'So how else am I to find I job?" I hear you ask.

The Right Way to Determine the Next Step in Your Career

It's not about finding a job. It's about finding the right place in the workforce and world—for you. Not for anyone else.

Your place in the world is important. This isn't about what you do, it's about who you are. Again: we are human beings, not human doings. When you live in the genius of who you are, you thrive. When you try to fit yourself into what others want you to be, well, not so much. It's about who you want to be.

So how does this work?

I created the Love, Lead, Live model, which has worked wonders for me and many others.

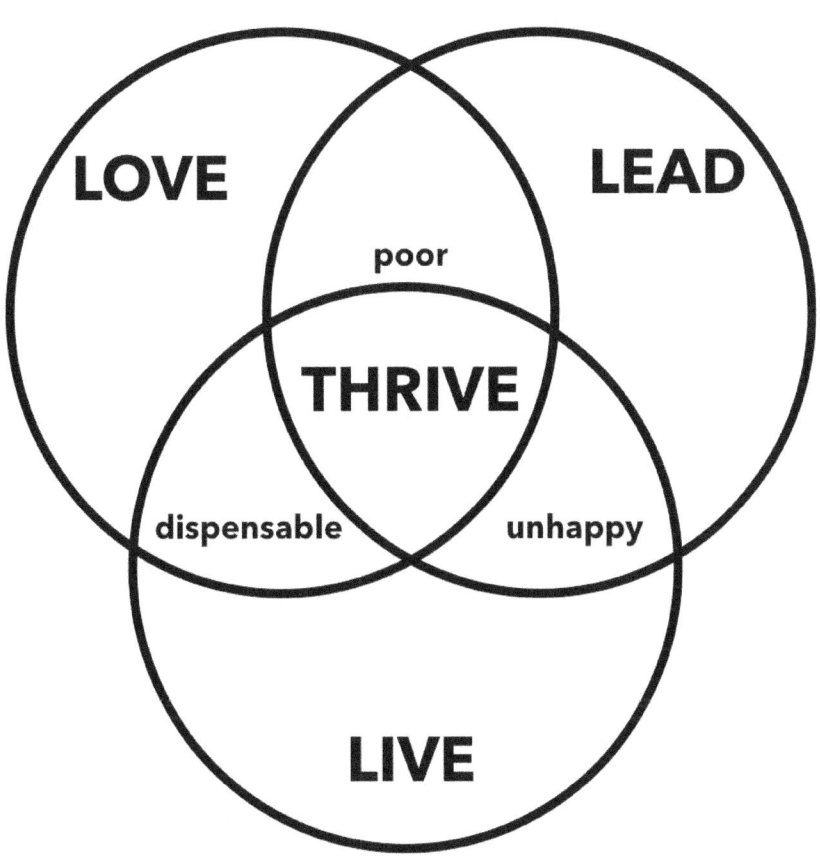

It's best visualized using three overlapping circles and can be seen in the accompanying illustration. Love. Lead. Live.

Love. This is, naturally, what you love. "Love what you do and the money will follow" is a popular saying. But love is only the beginning. I loved partying when I was younger, and the money didn't follow. It fled! Love is just the first step.

Lead. Lead is the second step. Lead is leadership. And this isn't about leadership in the way it's often bandied about as only important in the C-Suite. This is about what you do that others come to you for. It's about being best in the world at something, whether that's being the best occupational assessment trainer in your local municipal employment office, or the greatest quarterback of all time, or the most meticulous collar presser in Duluth. It's about you being the go-to person for something. It's about being indispensable in some leadership way.

Live. Live is about what people will pay you to do. Once you fill in the first couple circles, you'll see this isn't as big a deal as you may think. That old question, "You mean people actually get paid to do that?" can come true for you.

The whole model comes together in the center—the Thrive spot.

If you love and lead, but don't live, you'll live in poverty.

If you lead and live, but don't love, you'll be miserable.

If you live and love, but don't lead, you're replaceable, expendable.

When all three combine: That's where you Thrive. That's who you are.

When we love what we do, earn more than we need, make the world a better place, we simply enjoy life better. That's when you start rating your whole life -- including how you spend the majority of your waking hours — as a 10!

The rest of this book is designed to take you through the process of getting you to that sweet Thrive spot — and staying there!

How This Book Works For You

Each chapter is filled with models, tools, exercises, and concrete, simple action steps to get you to the career—and life—you can only dream about right now.

In Chapter One: Love, we'll give you a secret tool for finding out what you truly love. It's not as clear-cut as it may seem. In fact, I wish I'd had

How happy
are you
in your current job?

10   **LOVE IT!!!!**

9

8

7

6

5

4

3

2

1   **HATE IT!!!**

this tool decades ago; it would have cut years off my struggle to find the perfect career for me. In this chapter, we'll also identify what is blocking you from getting where you want to go. You know that old saying that we are sometimes our own worst enemy, or that the biggest obstacle to your success is you? Yep. In this chapter we identify all the stinking thinking and habits that prevent us from finding true happiness. Lastly in this chapter we offer simple action steps to get the whole process in motion.

In Chapter Two: Lead, we identify areas where you excel. We take the blocks identified in the first chapter and break them down, clearing a path to success. We also provide a clear strategy to find a way to mix and match what you love with what you're good at. This way will lead you to greater income, career satisfaction, and fulfillment.

In Chapter Three: Live, we zero in on what you can get paid for — and paid handsomely! We build on the strategy from chapter two to help you create an easy action plan.

In Chapter Four: Thrive, everything comes together. Not only will you have everything you need to get your current career on a new high, you'll get the tools for ensuring that you're never stuck in a bad job again.

Where Are You At Now?

Before we dive in, let's rate where you are now.

On a scale of 1 to 10 — 10 being completely happy, 1 being miserable — where do you rate on career satisfaction? Be honest with yourself.

[GRAPHIC - 1-10 Satisfaction scale]

2? 6? 7? 5? 8? 9? 3?

How would your life, indeed your world, change if you were 10-happy with your job?

How would your relationships with your family and children and friends change?

How would your mood be different when you rise every morning be different?

How might your diet and exercise routine change if you weren't expending so much energy just trying to suffer through another laborious project at work that your heart is just not into?

What would your world look like if you loved what you do during the greater part of your waking hours?

Keep that image in mind as you work your way through this book.

This image can be a reality!

Come along!

1

LOVE

"The world is full of unsuccessful businessmen who still secretly believe they were meant to be artists or writers or actors in movies."
— Thomas Merton

"Do what you love and the money will follow," has become a popular career development watch cry.

If I might be frank, there was a period in my life when I LOVED dancing, drinking, and going to nightclubs—having a lot fun. The money never followed. It fled!

I loved playwriting too—still do—and I tried my hand at that for years, but no money followed. I labored long and hard, paying other people to help me learn the craft better and to stage readings of my work and more. I think I got a $50 check, once, for one of my creations.

Don't get me wrong. Doing what you love is very important. People who are passionate about their work are far more likely to be successful and happy than those who are not.

But if you listen deeply to those who love what they do for a living, there's something more than action. A huge part of what makes them in love with their living is that they are living out what they value.

My dear friend Michael Kuchwara knew instinctively what he wanted to do with his life from a very young age. He wanted to be a theater critic. And he became one, an outstanding one. He spent a full career writing theater reviews for the Associated Press. His love for his work was infectious. He did his job so well and was so well loved, that when he passed away at an untimely early death in his 50s, Broadway dimmed its lights in his honor. And while Broadway has dimmed its lights at the passing of many great actors and performers, this was the first for a theatrical critic. I spent a lot of time with Michael. And I can tell you that he loved, loved, loved his work. It fulfilled just about all of the values he held dear. He valued creative expression—his own and others. He valued being in the know, a well-turned phrase, being adored, and great achievement. He instinctively knew how to combine these into an extraordinary career.

Most of us aren't so fortunate to know precisely how to make a living that honors our values. I haven't been.

Many of us need to think a little more deeply and be a bit more intentional.

And that's where this Love exercise can be a big help.

The Love Exercise

I discovered this exercise late in life. Knowing of it earlier would have saved me a lot of time, energy, money, and headaches.

This tool is one of the best ways I know to access values in our lives that we truly love.

In order to do it most effectively, I encourage you to find a quiet place to sit and relax. Close your eyes, take a breath and begin to think about where you would like your life to be in twenty years. What would you like to have accomplished? Think about it in the present tense. So think about it as Wednesday January 27, 2037. What does your life look like?

Think about what our life would look like in twenty years. This may seem odd to you because when we talk about careers we often say where do you want to be in five years or ten years? I'm asking for twenty years. Before I tell you why let me explain the exercise a little more.

Where are you living? What are you doing for leisure? What are the

<u>LOVE</u>
What would you like your life to look like in 20 years?

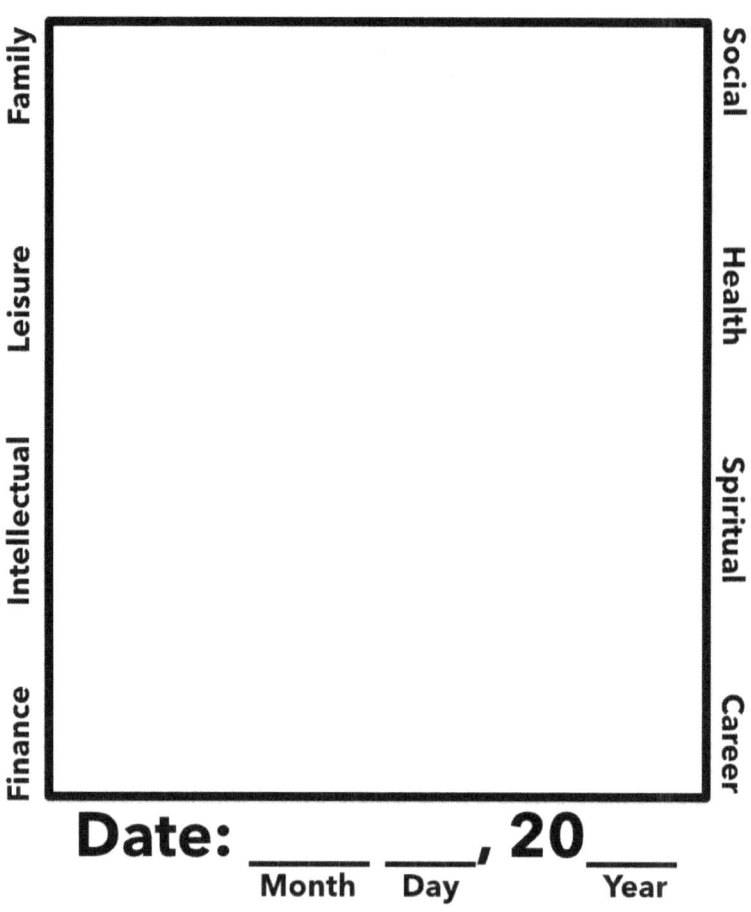

Family   Leisure   Intellectual   Finance

Social   Health   Spiritual   Career

Date: _____ ___, 20___

Month   Day   Year

intellectual pursuits you are engaged in? What have you accomplished? Have you perhaps written a book? Do you have a family? Children? Grandchildren? What is your social life like? How's your health? Where are you living? Are you near the sea? Do you have a second home? What's your career like?

We are not just looking for career. It is important to get the whole picture. What is your social life like? What does your financial situation look like? How much money do yo have saved and invested? What is your ideal vision for twenty years from now?

I encourage you to spend time with it, dream and love it, enjoy it. Really go with it. Make this a fun exercise.

Take out a sheet of paper and write the date twenty years from now on it. Then write down everything you came up with in the present tense. You can check out the illustration for an example of a template to use.

So why do we go out twenty years? For five years out you can pretty much set goals. For ten years it's difficult to set benchmarks and timeline. Twenty years out, it is almost impossible to lay out a concrete plan of action. It's just too far in the future with too many unknown and unexpected variables. We want to look at twenty years because that's really a dream. We want to get away from asking ourselves: How will I achieve this? We just want to live in the dream.

We are after this dream vision because when you dream about that future, it really gets at who you are and what is important to you.

What really motivates you? What things are most important to you? That's where the dreaming comes in. What you dream, divorced from concrete planning, is what excites you. This is what you love.

Here's some of what I have in my vision (remember, it's in present tense, as if I'm living this twenty years hence) :

"I have written several books. I travel the world giving talks and presentations as a thought leader in how people can manage themselves to create the type of lives and world they want. I am running a great company where I help lots of people to create opportunities for themselves—to love live and lead in the world. I am financially stable, with more than enough savings to retire comfortably—if I choose to retire. (Though I'm loving my work so much I can't imagine retiring!) I am on the boards of a couple of stellar non-profit institutions that are making amazing differences in the world. My social calendar is filled with interesting events and activities with fascinating people and friends and family who I love. I love my regular weekend trips to the mountains. It's kinda silly, but I loved my recent trip to an over-the-top resort in Dubai. I go on retreat twice a year to revitalize my spiritual well-being. I meditate, pray, and exercise regularly, and I eat right with lots of vegetables and lean meat."

That's the idea.

Once you have your vision down, take a look at it. Read through it. Breathe it in. Really enjoy it.

Next, we're going to tease out the values that are embedded in that vision.

Values are the beginning of this whole process. Getting the values right is critical because being happy is, again, not about what we do.

We get very hung up on "Should I be a software engineer? Should I be a fireman? Should I be a chef? Should I be this? Should I be a blacksmith?"—Yes, blacksmith.— That's right, blacksmiths don't exist anymore (except, for the most part, in historic showplaces like Plimouth Plantation). Again, it's not about what you do. Occupations like blacksmith come and go. But if you were a Colonial blacksmith and were being downsized as the industrial revolution barrels through town, you'd be able to use your values to lead you to the next best career opportunity. Values set the foundation for what we love and who we are.

When I did this values work a while ago, I was trying to figure out my own career path. My vision, as you can see from above, included travel, speaking, writing books and such. From that vision, I came up with a list of values. Then I ranked them. Discerned through my 20 year vision, my top value at that time turned out to be freedom. At the time, I was saddled a nine-to-five job. I discovered that my value around freedom, unbeknownst to my conscious self, had risen higher than my value around financial security. So I gleaned something very important about myself: To be happy, I needed to think about jobs where I had more freedom. That's how I ended up where I'm at now, and writing this book!

Sometimes values come into conflict. So you will want to prioritize them to some degree. I do this with my coach. Just as in my example, freedom can come into conflict with financial security.

Take a stab at creating your values from your vision. Write them down. Then insert those values in the Love circle of your Love Lead Live diagram.

This is what you value right now. This may shift. But at least you have criteria by which to start judging career opportunities that come your way. I continually use my values list to determine if an opportunity is right for me.

For instance, sometimes a big money job opportunity comes my way and I get all excited with dollar signs in my eyes! But when I run the opportunity through my ranked values, I sometimes find that big money conflicts with things I value more highly, like freedom. Sometimes it doesn't. But I know I spent a lot of time in my twenties chasing jobs on Wall Street that didn't satisfy me simply because the money seemed so good. It made me miserable. Today, I earn more than I need, and I'm happier.

So go ahead and write down your values and rank them. Again, don't obsess about it. You can change them later. Just set the baseline. You'll be glad you did.

More about Your Vision

Here's a bonus about the vision you created.

Your vision is very powerful in its own right. You don't even have to cull the values from it. Take your created vision and use it as a personal advertisement for yourself. I have my 20-year vision posted over my desk!

We know from neuroscience that what you visualize, you more easily create in your life. The more I have the vision of the life I want in front of me, the more I subconsciously create that vision.

We know how advertising works. Once a commercial is in front of us 26 times or so—called "the effective frequency rate"—we're buying a product. I may find myself unthinkingly purchasing Tide detergent at my local grocery store. Why Tide over every other brand? Because my brain neurology has been trained by those ads to zero in on Tide. Why does Tide spend money on advertising? Because it works. So Proctor & Gamble is advertising its Tide agenda to me, nudging me to do what P&G wants me to do—buy Tide.

You want to do the same thing with your vision. You want to sell yourself on the vision you want for your future life. You want to place it in front of yourself in a compelling, advertising-like way, over and over, until you are unconsciously "buying" your vision—that is, doing everything we can to make that vision a reality in your life.

Your vision is your advertisement to yourself. Use it. Find ways to keep flashing it in front of you. Just like a Tide detergent commercial, the more you put your vision in front of you, the more you'll re-orient and re-organize your life to achieve and buy that as your life.

I encourage you to post your vision in different places—by your bedside, what have you. (I set mine as my home screen on my smartphone!

Every time I get a phone call the image of a book on career flashes in front of me. It reminds me to write the book you're reading now. It really works!) Before you know it—voila!—you'll be living the life you envisioned not long ago.

What's Stopping You?!—Part I

Obstacles. Blocks.

What is getting in the way of you getting into a career you love?

I know. Yuck!

This is where we really want to look at what the ugly voices in your head are saying:

"Ugh, I can never get a job that pays me enough." "I am making a lot of money and it is miserable, but you know I've got a mortgage, I've got these bills, and on and on." Or "You are too old to change careers." Or "I'm too young." "I don't have enough experience to really get where I want." "Nobody takes me seriously so why should I bother?"

You want to think about those negative thoughts, and get them all down on paper, in front of you. They sound terrible in your head. They're even uglier on paper!

You can't deal with the block if you can't see the block. It's really hard to remove a branch blocking your path if you can't see it well. It's difficult to get around a boulder in a river bed that's blocking your boat if you don't have a sense of its size and shape. You want to get clear on what the nasty voices in our head are saying. Only then can you confront them head on.

These negative voices are what keep you from really getting where you want.

Here's one of the biggest blocks I hear about, especially after people complete the vision exercise:

It's great to see that amazing possible future, but how can I ever hope to achieve it? It's like seeing the Promised Land, but The Red Sea is in the way. It looks insurmountable. How do I get there?"

I'm no Moses, but this process I'm about to share with you will help you begin to remove those barriers—no miraculous parting of huge waterways necessary.

All of these blocks are limiting-beliefs running around in our heads. They put limits and restrictions on us.

Beliefs are extraordinarily powerful. And limiting-beliefs are the number one obstacle between you and the job of your dreams. They imprison you. The are ruining your life and keeping you stuck.

I got my master's degree from the Divinity School at Harvard University. I know a little about belief.

Belief is one of the most powerful forces in the universe. Beliefs can cause wars or they can create miracles. Think about a time when you really believed you could do something. Nothing could stop you. Think of "The Little Engine that Could": "I think I can. I think I can. I think I can. I know I can. I know I can. I know I can!" When you really believe you can do something, there's nothing that can stop you.

Belief is one of the few forces that can override the fundamental, natural desire for self-preservation. Look at the martyrs. Their beliefs compels them to let themselves be killed and to die. It is belief that allows them to sacrifice their very lives.

So why not engage in a belief that doesn't lead to sacrificing your life. How about a belief that creates a life beyond your wildest dreams? Belief can do that.

I had a client who truly believed no one really loved his work. He had to have that belief profoundly challenged. When he opened up to a new belief—to the possibility that people could love their work and that he could too—he ended up working at a place where everyone loves their job.

It's not magic or even religion. Neuroscience is proving that the power of what we think and believe can radically transform our lives.

Changing your limiting-beliefs is the difference between you watching the clock, miserable, hating your co-workers — and true happiness.

True happiness! You ready for that? I think I hear a few yeses, and maybe an Amen!

It all begins with facing those negative thoughts floating around in your head. Get them onto paper now. We'll begin to transform them in the next chapter. For now, get clear on how many awful voices there are.

Act Now!—Part I

It's well and good to sit around dreaming about the kind of life you'd love to live. And it's really great to do introspective work to find out what those detrimental voices are saying about the prospect of achieving that kind of life. But if you're actually going to realize that vision, you have to get into action.

That means interacting with people. The simple secret of making a career transition?: It's more important to look for people than to look for a job. That's right. Think about it. Companies don't hire people. People hire people. When you get hired, it will be because someone—an actual person—will okay your hiring.

To have a great career—even if its doing introverted work like writing—you're going to have to interact at some point and in some way with people.

This can be a very uncomfortable part of the career transition process, particularly if you have introverted tendencies like I do. So we want to start by getting into the habit of connecting with other people—as soon as possible. And we want to make it as enjoyable as possible too.

We can do it in any number of ways. It could be by email, by phone, by text, through networking events, or through any myriad of methods. But we need to do it.

In fact, meeting people can be fun. And if it's not, then go write down all the negative thoughts you have about networking and meeting people in the Blocks exercise. Get those down on paper too!

The first Action exercise is to simply make a list of twenty people to talk with about the career transition you're going through.

Perhaps your uncle, your neighbor, or your best friend. It doesn't really matter right now. It does not have to be anyone you think will lead you to your dream job right now. For the moment, simply make a list of people whom you want to tell about your job search, your dreams, and your vision. That's it!

And make a list of twenty. We'll explain why twenty later. For now, just make the list. Begin by thinking about people you can talk with about what you are looking for in our job. If you can't come up with 20 people, ask some of the first people on your list for more names.

Look on LinkedIn. You may see someone and say to yourself: "Oh my goodness; that is a person whom I have always admired who does work I might like to do!" You don't have to worry about reaching out to them, which might be scary at this point. Just put them on the list for now. If you want to reach out, that's even better. Reaching out is the kind of action we want to make into a habit. The saying that "your network is your net worth" is about finding our way into the place where we're going to Thrive.

A powerful question someone asked me when I started my business was: "Where can you find your ideal client in abundance cheaply and easily?" I would rephrase that in the same way for career. "Where can you find an abundance of people who can lead you to your dream career?" Those are the people you want to put on your list.

Next

As you get clearer on what you really value and love, and as you work through your internal blocks and get into the habit of talking with people about where you want to go, you'll start to make major progress toward actually creating the beautiful life you set down in your vision.

In the next chapter we'll look at actual skills and leadership abilities that you bring to your career search. We'll also turn around those nasty statements going through your head. And we'll look at more ways to get you into networking and connecting with other people so you can get that career you dream about ASAP.

2

Lead

"Whether we like it or not, the call of our generation is not to occupy positions created for us, but ... to create positions for ourselves."
— *Clair Chase*

Quick: What's the best place to get a pastrami-on-rye sandwich in New York?

Just about anyone from the Big Apple will tell you Katz's Deli on the Lower East side. (Also famous for a certain scene from "When Harry Met Sally.")

What's the best person from which to find out about Roman Catholicism?

The pope, of course.

Who is the go-to mechanic in your neighborhood?

Who is the person in your office who is most likely to know who is sleeping with whom?

Who is the person in your office you go to when you really need to get something done and done quick and well?

Who is the person you go to when you need to better understand office politics?

The Lead Exercise

In the last chapter you assessed what you Love, what you value.

In this chapter, we look at Lead, which is, in many ways, about what others love about us.

Leading is about what people come to us for, what we can be best in the world at. Leading is about what we do really well. It's like when people say:

"You want a presentation done right? Then you need to go to Cindy in the marketing department. She knows how to make a slideshow really pop."

We want to come up with a full list of what brings you top of mind to others. What follows is the best activity I have found for doing this. It's called an Achievements–to-Skills Worksheet.

You first want to create a worksheet with three columns. Feel free to follow along in the included illustration. The first column holds the title "What." That's where you want to come up with a list of your top ten accomplishments in life. They could be job related, or school projects, or an extracurricular activity. It could be that you solved the Rubik's Cube in record time at your school, or you raised a daughter, or you sequenced DNA for an earthworm for the first time.

For example, one of my biggest accomplishments was directing a school play. Another major achievement was that I created the first online cross-cultural, multi-national security services information sharing online digital presence for Citibank Worldwide Securities Services. I worked with people in Singapore, and Europe, all over the world in 62 different countries. So you see, it doesn't really matter how big or small the job, it's an accomplishment. So we want to think about something that you've done. In the first column, list your achievements.

In the second column, called 'What You Did,' write down more fully what it is you did. For my example 'directed a school play,' I put in the second column that: I created a vision, organized people and ideas into a coherent event, and led the team to a triumph.

Here's another example, if a first column entry was about how I project-managed a huge biotech product to FDA approval, I might write this in the second column: "I got people all on the same page. I kept people on

LEAD

What valuable skills do you possess?

	I - What	II - What You Did	III - Skills
example	Directed school play	Created a vision. Organized people & ideas into a coherent event. Led team to triumph!	Vision, Organization, Creation, Events, Leadership, Teamwork.
1			
2			
3			
4			
5			
6			
7			
8			
9			
10			

deadlines in teams on multiple continents. I managed cultural tensions. I maintained accountability across all team leads. I was able to translate complicated biotechnical language into meaningful and useful instructions for non-biotechnical marketers and other team members." And so on.

Just write it all out. Don't over think and make a big deal out of it. Do some free writing. Just set the story down on paper.

Next—again without much thinking—circle the action verbs.

For instance, in the illustrated example, I circled "created," and "vision," and so on.

What we are doing is taking the narrative out. We're trying to identify particular skills from a story you have about them in your head. This is critical.

If you continue to think that "translate complicated biotechnical language into meaningful and useful instructions for non-biotechnical marketers" will only work in the context of work at a pharmaceutical company, then you are limiting your options. If you circle the verb "translate" you begin to see your skills in a new light. It may not be that your expertise is just in biotech. It could be your real brilliance is in your ability to bridge the gap between how marketers speak, how engineers speak, how business people speak, and how the legal team speaks. You may have valuable skills in inter-departmental communications. That opens you up to career possibilities in whole new realms.

Consider one of my clients who thought he could only work in publishing. He confided in me that he couldn't imagine being happy in the publishing industry again. He was too burned out there. We discovered that in building his department at the publisher, he had actually created a whole business unit. He had business-building skills. It was that opening that allowed him to shift into a completely different career.

So circle the verbs and skills in the second column and then write what you circled in the third column. For instance, for play directing, in column three I came up with: "vision, organization, creation, events, leadership, teamwork."

Look at those words in column three again:

Vision.

Organization.

Creation.

Events.

Leadership.

Teamwork.

When you see those together. What's the first thought that springs to mind? Probably not "directed a school play."

This is where things get exciting.

Values + Skills = New Opportunities

Write each one of those skills on a separate index card.

Then go back to the Love circle and look at the values you wrote there. Write those values on separate index cards.

Now, literally, throw all those index cards on your floor! Mix them up. Forget where they came from!

Then get down and start to move the cards around and see how they randomly come together. Perhaps the cards for leadership, team, freedom, and achievement all congregate. Consider what jobs might fit that; perhaps CEO of a small startup.

Start playing with all those cards! We'll do more with this in the next chapter. Don't move ahead too quickly. Really have fun tossing the cards around and daydreaming. Bring in your partner or friends to help you brainstorm. Yay!

Next, come up with a list of at least twenty different possible new and different occupations. I like lists of twenty, because twenty is a difficult number to get at when you're brainstorming. You begin to peter out around ten, and then at fifteen you tend to become frustrated. It's after that point that you start to break through to really unconventional possibilities. These open doors to opportunities you never would have dreamed of, and that could actually unlock the secret to creating your dream career. Go deep. Go broad. Come up with a list of 40 or more if you can. The more you put in, as the saying goes, the more you'll get out of it.

And what if you get stuck?

Let's pick up where we left off from the last chapter concerning blocks.

What's Stopping You?!—Part II

In the last chapter we asked you to come up with a list of negative thoughts, things that are getting in your way.

If you haven't already, I really encourage you to write down all those nasty horrible voices that are running through your head saying you aren't good enough, or you're too old for a job change, or whatever it is that is keeping you from taking action to get you to a career you love.

Here's one block a student in one of our career classes came up with:

"This is too much trouble. I just want to stay in bed."

That's a great block and certainly one I've encountered.

One of the biggest blocks I had when thinking about starting this coaching business and helping people with their careers, was:

"James you can't possibly start your own business, you've never sold anything in your life."

That voice kept me saying, "Just don't bother doing it, because it's a waste of time, it's going to take you forever, you've never been a salesperson, this is just the most ridiculous thing, you just need to stay in a nine to five job in a cubicle," and so on and on and on. Every time I started to think, "I can start to do this, I'm excited about it," the voice would say, "No, you can't do that because you've never sold anything in your life."

It's very important to identify all the voices. Then find the ones you have the most negative energy around. Some of the voices in my head would say, "I'm too tired." That's a powerful voice. But is that the MOST powerful voice keeping me from getting where I want to go?

Play around with some of the voices and rewrite them until you come up with the most powerful negative statement blocking you from moving forward from finding a career you'll love.

Now we're going to take that one negative thought and turn it from being your biggest obstacle to becoming your greatest asset. I call this Belief Alchemy. It's put together by a coaching colleague of mine, Jonathan (Jeb) Bates.

It's a six part process.

(1) First, identify the current belief that's holding you back.

I'll use my belief as an example:

Belief Alchemy

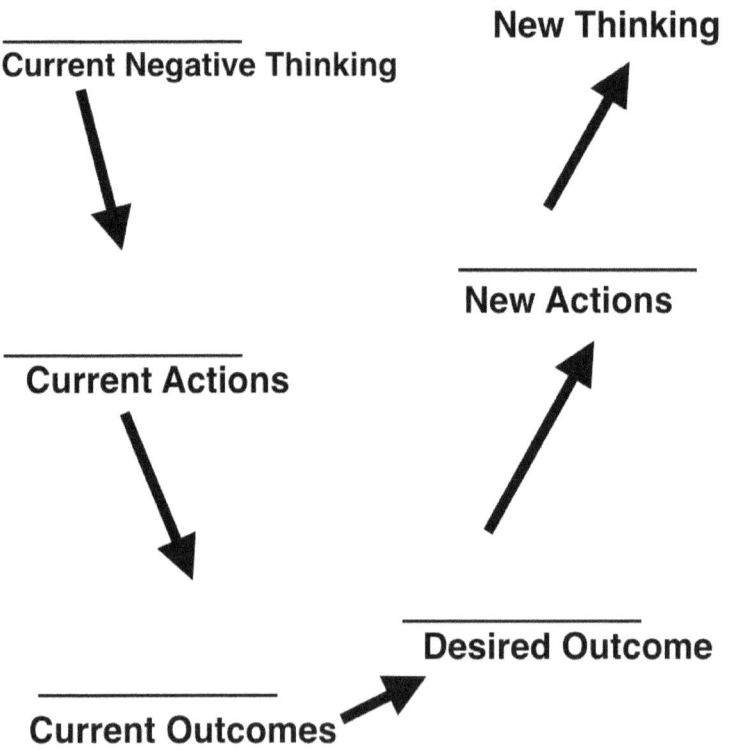

Current Negative Thinking

Current Actions

Current Outcomes

New Thinking

New Actions

Desired Outcome

* adapted from a process from The Results System™*

"James you can't possibly start your own business, you've never sold anything in your life."

(2) Second ask yourself is what action does that belief lead to? What that action led to for me was no action at all.

(3) Then we ask ourselves in the third part, what's the outcome of that action, or in my case, of that inaction? The outcome of that action for me was nothing. Actually there's always an outcome. For me, it wasn't a nothing outcome, my outcome was that I remained miserable.

I saw a great saying on my Facebook feed recently: "Sometimes the Riskiest Thing You Can Do Is Not Do Anything At All." That's what I was doing—nothing. That was a huge risk because I was getting more miserable with each passing day. Not only were things not staying the same, they were getting worse.

(4) Next, in the fourth part, ask yourself what's your desired outcome? My desired outcome was to create a business where I was helping people to get better lives and better jobs.

(5) Fifth, ask yourself what action do you need to take to achieve that desired outcome? I realized I needed to remind myself that other people have started businesses before, other people have built businesses helping people get into other positions in life that are happier. And the first action I needed was to find those people and ask how they did it—to learn from them. Sure I'd never built a business before but there are a lot of things I've never done in my life. At one point, I didn't know how to ride a bike, I didn't know how to dance. I learned how to do both. I can learn how to do this too. I can learn how to build a business.

(6) So the sixth part of Belief Alchemy is to come up with the new thinking you need to propel yourself into the action you decided you needed to take in part five. The new thought I came up with was:

"James you've always been a great learner. You can learn how to create a business, you can find out how to make money at this, you can do this!"

That was very powerful. It's why you're holding this book in your hands right now.

Without that new thinking, I'd still be stuck with that old belief going through my head, "You'll never sell anything, this is just useless."

I wouldn't be doing what I'm doing today. And you wouldn't be getting these suggestions.

Act Now!—Part II

As you continue to gain insight about what you Love, discover the great skills you can Lead with, and work through your blocks, you also need to continue being very active in your career process.

In the action part of the last chapter, I asked you to come up with a list of twenty people.

Remember from earlier: (1) that 80% of jobs are not posted publicly; it takes knowing other people to discover them, and (2) companies don't hire people, people hire people.

And, yes, it's a list of twenty again. There's another reason why twenty or more is particularly powerful when it comes to listing people. The people you know in your immediate inner circle already know practically everything about you. And you know practically everything about them. They're not likely to lead you to your dream job. It's the people just beyond them that often prove the most valuable in a career search. Once you get past that first circle, you're going to be wracking your brain more.

What I encourage people to do, if they're struggling coming up with twenty, is to ask other people to help expand the list. Working this exercise hard forces you into new territory. This is when you start to come up with things that you never would have thought of before, when you begin to have breakthroughs and experience great progress.

Further, when you look at your list, ask yourself: what are some things about those people and what they do or have done that excites you?

Another reason to look for people rather than jobs is when you look for people it opens up the possibility of learning what a human being actually does. Recall: We're human beings, not human doings. When we think: "They're really interesting. I'd love to learn more about what they do," it begins with them as human beings, not what they do.

This was powerfully brought home to me while working with a client. After looking at his list, he realized the people who most fascinated him were all doing communications and press relations work. My client was doing fundraising and event planning. Though the thought of a career in communications had passed lightly through his head, he'd never seriously considered it. Whole new vistas opened up in his career search.

Action leads to insight. Even though action seems very tedious, the more we act, the more we're going to learn.

Now, with your list of interesting people to reach out to in hand, narrow it down to about four or five with whom you would really like to talk about making some sort of change in your career.

From that list of four or five, choose one person.

Then reach out to them.

This isn't always easy.

I have an illustration and instructions for how to reach out. I know this from working with others, and also from my own experience.

Sometimes I get caught up with this, we all get caught up in this. "How do I just reach out to somebody?" Let's make it easy. Here's an example of how I do it. You can also follow along in the illustration.

Begin with a personal opener that's your voice, that's kind of fun. For example:

(1) "Dear Tom,

"It's been a loooooong time!"

(2) Next:

"I saw on LinkedIn you've got a great new gig, very excited for you."

This second part consists of saying something that's personalized for them so they know you're focused on them and that this isn't a form letter.

(3) Third element: get as quickly as possible to the ask.

"I'd love to pick your brain on career possibilities."

(4) The next element is to tell them what you might provide.

"I'd love to buy you a cup of coffee, or lunch." Or:

"I may have some leads for you."

(5) Then make a friendly closing:

"I hope you're enjoying this April snowstorm! LOL. I look forward to being in touch! Thanks!"

Don't obsess over it. Just reach out. And if you get all negative in the head about it, then activate your Belief Alchemy.

Remember, you're aiming for a career that you're gonna really love. Let that dream vision motivate you!

The good news, is that the more you reach out the easier it gets. And that's what the next chapter covers in more detail.

3

LIVE

"I have not failed, I've just found 10,000 ways that won't work."
— Thomas Edison

Remember the index cards exercise?

Take your lists of values and skills and write each of them on an index card. Mix them up and match them in different ways and see what you come with. Think of job possibilities that arise from the different combinations. Write down at least twenty of them.

One of my clients, we'll call him Tony, gave me a call after throwing his values and skills index cards in the air and making that long list. Following years of being more than fed up with his job, Tony was open to something completely different. He began reading his twenty.

"Recruiter," he read first. "But that's the last thing I want to do."

"Okay," I told him. "Great. You don't have to do that. After you read your entire list, I'm going to ask you to choose one that sounds most interesting to you right now. It doesn't have to be recruiter. What's next on your list?"

He read through the rest of the possibilities. And after a bit of discussion, he decided that running his own business held the most excitement for him.

A couple of months later he enthusiastically accepted a job as—of all things—a recruiter.

How in the heck did that happen?

That's what this chapter is all about. We offer you a simple process for iterating toward a job that you'll love and earns you more than you need. And where you end up may completely surprise you!

Yes, we're asking you to review your list of twenty job possibilities from the last chapter. Pick one that excites you or at least seems to be one that could move you toward a job you could be happy in. Don't make a big deal out of it. We're not asking you to choose your next career and what you'll be doing for the next 80 years. Just what you might want to do next in life. Like in the story that began this chapter, you may end up with something completely different in a very short time. So don't obsess about the choice. Go with something for now.

This is your best guess for your next job. We call this your career hypothesis,

And just like your high school science experiments we will want to test your hypothesis.

Crank Up Your Career

This scientific process for figuring out your next career is what I call the Hypo Test Process. It consists of three parts: (1) Hypothesis, (2) Test, and (3) Process. Hypo, Test, Process.

You can follow along in the illustration if you like. Using this process took this chapter's hero, Tony, from a miserable job he was stuck in for many years to job happiness in just a couple of months. In fact, even though Tony began with the hypothesis of a new career running his own business, he actually cycled through several hypothetical career choices in a matter of weeks before landing his recruiting gig. One of his hypotheses was a career as a real estate agent. That also happened to be the career hypothesis of another client of mine.

Let's use real estate agent to take us through the Hypo Test Process.

Hypothesis

This other client—we'll call her Latisha—thought that being a real estate agent could satisfy her desires for socializing, community and freedom. Her go-to skills as someone who knows neighborhoods and the value of buildings (she was working in the insurance industry at the time.) She felt that this would also make her good at real estate.

STRATEGY

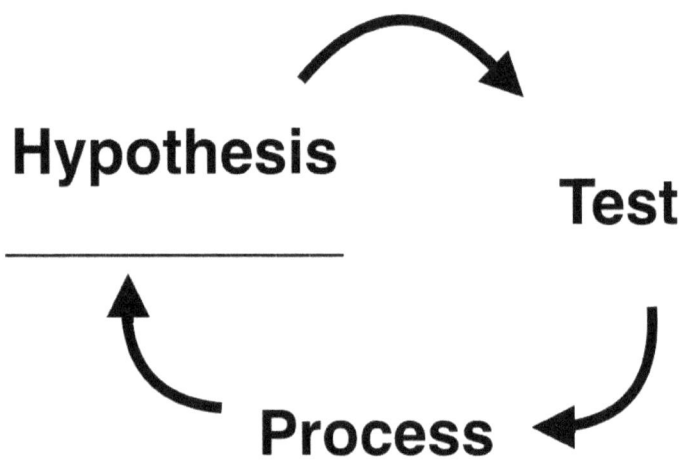

So her career hypothesis was real estate agent.

Test

Now we don't want to fall into a common trap. We don't want to determine if we want to go into real estate by thinking about it or reading about it, or Googling it, or watching movies like Glengarry Glen Ross. We don't conclude that the sun revolves around the earth simply because it looks like it does to us. We need to test our hypothesis.

A full-fledged test would be to go out and become a real estate agent and see if it feels right. But that's impractical, and a huge investment of energy and time.

So let's remember what we know from statistics. We can learn from a small sample more about the whole picture. So, how do we find a small sample?

You go into the field and investigate, like an anthropologist. You look for some real estate agents. You ask them what it's like to be an agent.

Think about it like a vacation destination. You can read and plan all you want about a trip to Italy. You can have all sorts of ideas about what it's like to be in Rome. When you get there, it's always different.

After you find a real estate professional, ask for 30 minutes of time to pick their brain about what they do. If you don't know any real estate agents —or people currently working in your hypothesized career path— then start asking all those on your list for people they know who work in that career or who might lead you to such people.

Keep talking.

The vast majority of people love to talk about their work. Grab coffee with them. Make it fun.

Ask them what a typical day looks like, what they like about their job, what they find frustrating.

When you go into the field and talk to real people doing real work, you get a much better idea of what a job is really like and whether it could really work for you.

Remember, we are looking for the right place for you.

With this newfound information, we move to part three: Process.

Process

Process, is where we decide if what we've learned about being a real estate agent, or whatever, makes us more interested or less interested in that career path.

Does it still meet our Love Lead Live criteria from the earlier chapters? In particular, does it align with your values. Ask yourself:

"Do I want to persevere in this direction or pivot to something else?"

Persevere or pivot?

Persevere could mean, "Yes, I still think I want to do real estate, but I just don't know where yet." In which case you begin doing more information interviews about location.

Or you may decide you now dislike the idea of real estate. In which case you go back to your list of twenty career possibilities and pick a new hypothesis. Or you may come up with new ideas.

You may even end up in a modified pivot, which is what happened to Latisha.

Latisha learned during her test phase that, while she liked the idea of real estate, she was worried about going into residential real estate in her area. There was a lot of competition there and it could take her years to reach the income level she wanted. Also, financial security was near the top of her values list.

Latisha was willing and able to take a monetary hit for a spell to be happier in how she made a living, but she got skittish about waiting several-years for the payoff. Fortunately, during her informational interviews, she discovered the world of corporate real estate. So she made a modified pivot, remaining with the real estate agent hypothesis, but investigating the possibility of being one for corporate buyers. With her corporate and insurance background, she learned that path might get her the kind of career she desired more quickly. So she took the commercial real estate agent career hypothesis through the Hypo Test Process.

And that's how it works.

Hypothesis. Test. Process: Pivot or Persevere. Hypo Test Process. Wash. Rinse. Repeat.

Do this process over and over and the job of your dreams will magically appear. You don't even have to think about it. Magic. Honest.

And since you're only looking into job ideas that sound exciting for you, it's a fun process.

And whenever doubt enters your head — "I can't possibly talk to another person" — or "I'll never be able to get my dream job" — or whatever limiting-belief comes up, simply work through your blocks as we did in the previous chapters. Transform those negative thoughts into a powerful belief to propel you to your dream career.

You deserve a career of your dreams. You deserve the best in this life. You deserve a standing ovation in this world.

Act Now!—Part III

You probably already guessed that the action step for this chapter is: start talking to people about your career hypothesis.

If you already know someone working in that job, reach out to that person. If you don't, start asking everyone you know if they have any ideas how to find someone who works in that profession.

Then, conduct a great information interview!

See the included illustration for some tips on how to conduct a great information interview.

Do it the way a young woman did with me recently. She reached out with a nice email, told me what she was up to, told me ways that she might be able to help me, dressed appropriately, and then asked a whole bunch of really interesting questions. That's it!

4

THRIVE

"Beginning every day with a positive action with my transition would be a great new routine."
— Deb, Career innerOvation class member

When do you want your amazing new job where you love what you do, and earn more than you need?

Three months from now? Six months from today? In two weeks?

Set an intention.

One of my clients set an intention to get a great new job in three months. Within a week a promising lead turned into gainful employment three-and-a-half months later.

Another client, who I started working with in December, decided he would have a great new job by the following March. And that's exactly what happened. Another decided she would have a great new gig in a month. Voila! 30 days later she had it!

Visualization and intention is extremely powerful. Of course it must also be accompanied with persistence.

Another client I began working with set an intention to find a new job in three months. After three weeks, other things distracted him. He started rescheduling appointments over and over until he just stopped coming. Two years later he was still in the same unhappy position.

Why did we wait until chapter four to talk about setting intentions? Ever hear the saying "Be careful what you wish for; you just might get it"? Exactly. When you set an intention and stick with it. It happens. So we want to be sure we are setting the right intentions.

Momentum

Now that you have all the pieces in place—Love Lead Live—you've worked through your biggest obstacles, and you're into action with the Hypo Test Process, it's now time to kick everything into high gear!

We've been through three chapters already. So let's do a quick recap before we get into the heart of this chapter's offerings: Thrive. Thriving is about action: taking everything we've done, all that foundational work, and then starting to turn it into, well, the metaphor I like to use is the fly wheel.

A fly wheel is the huge heavy stone in old mills. The stone wheel sat parallel to the ground on an axle, and they would connect horses to it. That's where we get the term, horsepower. It takes extraordinary energy from the horse to get that fly-wheel stone to turn just a fraction of an inch at first. The next fraction takes a little less horsepower and a little less energy. The next inch less, and the next even less, until the stone gets rolling. As the pace of the movement picks up, the incredibly heavy stone begins to roll on its own momentum. It starts turning so fast and with such power, that the horses need to be removed before they get pulled along faster than they can run and possibly stumble and get hurt.

That fly wheel process is an apt image of what happens between the moment we realize we are totally stuck in an unappealing career path and the moment when our career takes off on the wings of its own weight.

Think of this book as one of the horses helping to turn your wheel. Soon you won't need it. If you've been stuck in a career for a long time, it can take a lot of effort to simply move the wheel an inch or so. It can take a great deal of energy and dedication to fill out some of the exercises in these chapters. I'm also fond of the Abraham Lincoln quote, which I'm paraphrasing: "I walk slowly but I never walk backward." It's that sense of just one thing a day, every single day just taking a positive action, and the

ACTION

What are daily, weekly, and monthly actions to take?

DAILY ACTIONS GOALS

	Day 1	Day 2	Day 3	Day 4	Day 5	Day 6	Day 7	Day 8
Example: email 2 people	3	1	2	2	0	2	4	1

WEEKLY ACTION GOALS

	Week 1	Week 2	Week 3	Week 4	Week 5	Week 6	Week 7	Week 8
Example: 1 info interview	1	0	2	0	1	3	1	

MONTHLY ACTION GOALS

	Month 1	Month 2	Month 3	Month 4	Month 5	Month 6	Month 7	Month 8
Example: 2 networking events	3	1	2	1	0	2	2	2

cumulative effects of those actions build momentum.

To get a sense of that momentum, let's take a quick look at how far we have moved already.

At the beginning of the process you sought insight into what you Love, what you Lead in, and what you might be able to make a Living at—Love, Lead, Live. Along the way you identified negative thinking blocking you from that dream career and you turned those obstacles into motivational sayings. Discovering what you Love was about determining what you really value. You followed up by identifying what people come to you for—your skills—and the areas in which we can provide leadership: Lead. You mixed and matched our Love values and your Lead skills to help you brainstorm possible careers people might pay you for: Live.

After picking a career that particularly appealed to you, you made that into a career hypothesis. You tested that job hypothesis through information interviews with those actually engaged in that profession. Then you processed what you learned and decided if you wanted to keep looking at that career path, persevere, or pivot to another hypothesized career. Hypo Test Process.

Now you want to put the Hypo Test Process into hyper drive and give those fly wheel horses a run for their money. That takes action, and more action.

Again: since about eighty percent of available jobs are not advertised or posted anywhere, and since companies don't hire people, people hire people, the best way to find the right career path is to talk with people. Action in a career search primarily involves information interviewing. The Test part of the Hypo Test Process is about talking to people. It is arguably the most important part of the process. It's about getting out there, and finding out what's really happening on the ground.

One person I worked with thought she wanted do graphic design in the film industry because she thought there would be a lot of cool creativity in a film studio. After checking with people working in that profession, she discovered that in large movie production departments the creativity happens at the top. Lower level graphic designers take orders and have very little creative control, and it takes years or decades even to climb to a position where you can exert creative influence. Also, you're paid very little at first, and the entry level position churn rate is very high.

She asked one of the most important questions you can ask during an information interview: "Who else do you recommend I talk to?" Someone referred her to a graphic designer at a phone company. She was not initially excited about the prospect of working at a phone company. But when she talked to the employee who worked there, something clicked. This person made more at an entry level design position than those in Hollywood, and, while they had design constraints, they were afforded more creativity in their work. It was a revelation to learn that managers in a film studio were so creative that they would insist on their creative ideas thereby restrict creativity in their subordinates. In contrast, phone company managers, precisely because they were not creatively inclined, would allow more creativity to those they manage. That's the power of information interviewing.

Fail Fast

"I have not failed, I've just found 10,000 ways that won't work" is a famous Thomas Edison quote, and one of my favorites.

This Hypo Test Process is evidence-based. The best way to find something that works is to try as many ways as possible. Then rule out things we don't want as quickly as possible.

Edison used a lot of different platinum filaments to begin with. They kept burning no more than a few minutes. But he felt he was making some progress, so he persevered with platinum, until he just couldn't squeeze any more moments of illumination out of them. They weren't working long enough. So he made a pivot. He decided to try carbon filaments. He experimented with a bunch of types of carbon until he found this really obscure bamboo carbon from South America that suddenly burned a long time, and that's where he really got traction.

He kept trying different things, and kept ruling things out. That's what we do to find the perfect place for us, it's about ruling things out. Film and video may sound really exciting, but you begin to talk to people who are doing film and video editing in large companies like Sony, and you discover they're turnover mills for young creative people who largely burnout and don't move up. We perceive what a business is like because we watched a movie about it, but we don't really know until we talk to somebody who knows. That's why this strategy of testing and hypothesizing, and doing it as rapidly as possible, is really powerful.

When we get to our action worksheet, we may want to include a goal to go through a full Hypo Test Process once a week. We could determine to have a hypothesis about a job, have one information interview to test it, process the learning, and then decide to persevere or pivot to a new hypothesis by the end of that week. Thomas Edison has another famous quote I love: "Genius is 1% inspiration and 99% perspiration."

If we stay in action and keep ruling out job possibilities, then the right career is going to magically come to us. One of my clients found great freelance work doing her information interview process. She was simply talking to people when one of her interviewees asked her to help with some freelance creative work. This was not a job posted anywhere. This was a job out of a conversation. This is how we create jobs that we love.

Act Now!—Part IV

This chapter is all about action. Action is the power that gets this fly wheel into major motion. There are three tiers of actions that are helpful for getting us going: Daily actions, weekly actions, and monthly actions. Things that we can take on a daily basis could be as simple as one that came from a member of the career class we offer. It's just to do a positive thing each morning toward finding a dream career. Maybe it's just an affirmation. Or it could be to reach out to at least one person a day, through email or phone. Possible weekly actions include setting up at least one information interview per week. A person might want to set a goal of attending one networking event per week, or monthly. Some of us have full time jobs already, so we want to come up with something realistic. A monthly action could be just to join one professional group per month.

With your action items determined, put them on paper (see worksheet on page 38). Then add the timeframes and check them off as they get done.

Did I do it that morning? Yes or no? I can check it off. Post progress to Facebook. Did I informational interview two people? We want to make sure we track our actions, yet we want to give ourselves leeway. I like to say 80% is good enough. If eight out of ten days you follow up on LinkedIn, that's great. If you miss a day or two, not a big deal. 80% is perfect. And don't fret if it's below that. Any action in the right direction is action toward moving the fly wheel and gets you one action closer to career satisfaction.

It's getting the fly wheel going. In my experience if you do something every day, big things happen before you know it. This is how I've written books. My goal is to write something every day. Sometimes I go to bed and realize I haven't written anything. I sit up in bed, pull a pad of paper and just write one word, 'Book.' I wrote something about the book that day. Doing something small repeatedly eventually creates huge change. One or two days I'm only writing the word "book" but by the third day I'm writing a paragraph, then a page, then whole chapters at a time. It's how drops of water accumulate one drip at a time gradually transforming into huge currents and waterways that ground majestic mountains into piles of dirt at the end of river deltas. Small daily actions done over time are that powerful. It's the same thing with this career search —just a little bit every day, and eventually the fly wheel gets into motion.

EPILOGUE

HAPPILY EVER AFTER

Tony did it. Latisha did it. I did it. Brenda did it. Alex, Peter, Deb, Jerry, and countless others have done it. You can do it too!

A couple of years ago Rick came to me seeking relief from working for a corporation for over twenty years. The love fell out of that 'marriage' at about year twelve. Yikes! Eight years of job dissatisfaction. In short order Rick found himself in a rewarding position, taking a slight decrease in salary for the opportunity to assist at a company engaged in meaningful work. Jackpot! Thrive!

A year later he called me up. Something went wrong, he told me. Uh-oh, I thought. No, nothing terribly wrong, he said. The situation in his work environment had changed. He had a new boss. And one of the reasons he liked working at this new firm was how much he liked his former boss. This new boss, not so much. Other priorities were also shifting in his workplace. Nothing was horrible, yet. But that was the point. He didn't want things to get worse. He didn't want to find himself still miserable eight years later.

He pulled out the values clarification work that he and I had done earlier. In particular, he discovered his values around professional development and workplace improvement were not being met under his new manager. She focused far more on outcomes and deliverables. She didn't seem to care much about how things got done, only that they got done. Spending time figuring out how to improve work processes didn't seem to interest her. Rick had spent the better part of his year at the company developing a few of his team members who had been mediocre players for years, getting them promoted, helping them and the company. His new boss didn't seem to care. Rather than languish any longer, Rick wanted to take the work he'd done with me and start to apply it immediately to find the next best fit for him. And that's what he's doing.

Neither he nor I know where he will end up. As of this writing, he's still engaged in the process. (It's only been a few weeks.) But it's almost certain that if he remains engaged in this process it won't be eight years of misery again.

In fact, simply taking charge of the process of finding the next job that matches his values has already energized him.

Neurological studies demonstrate that just taking action in a certain direction can transform how we experience the world. Think about the last time you went on vacation. If you're like most people, you likely felt a little less stressed and a little more energized as soon as you scheduled the trip on your calendar. A little action goes a long way.

I like to say that everyone is their own CEO.

Take charge of your career as if you were your own CEO. Be the Chief Executive of your own life. Be like Rick. Don't just take whatever boss comes at you. Determine your own destiny. Determine what matters to you.

Get clear on what you Love.

Lead the world in what you're great at.

Live on the bounty the world provides for thriving in your genius.

It's as simple as that.

You'll earn more than you need.

You'll love what you do.

And you'll do the world a world of good.

I'm a firm believer that when everyone finds their Thrive spot we'll finally create the utopia that humanity has been searching for. Think about it. If everyone honored their true values and was doing work that they

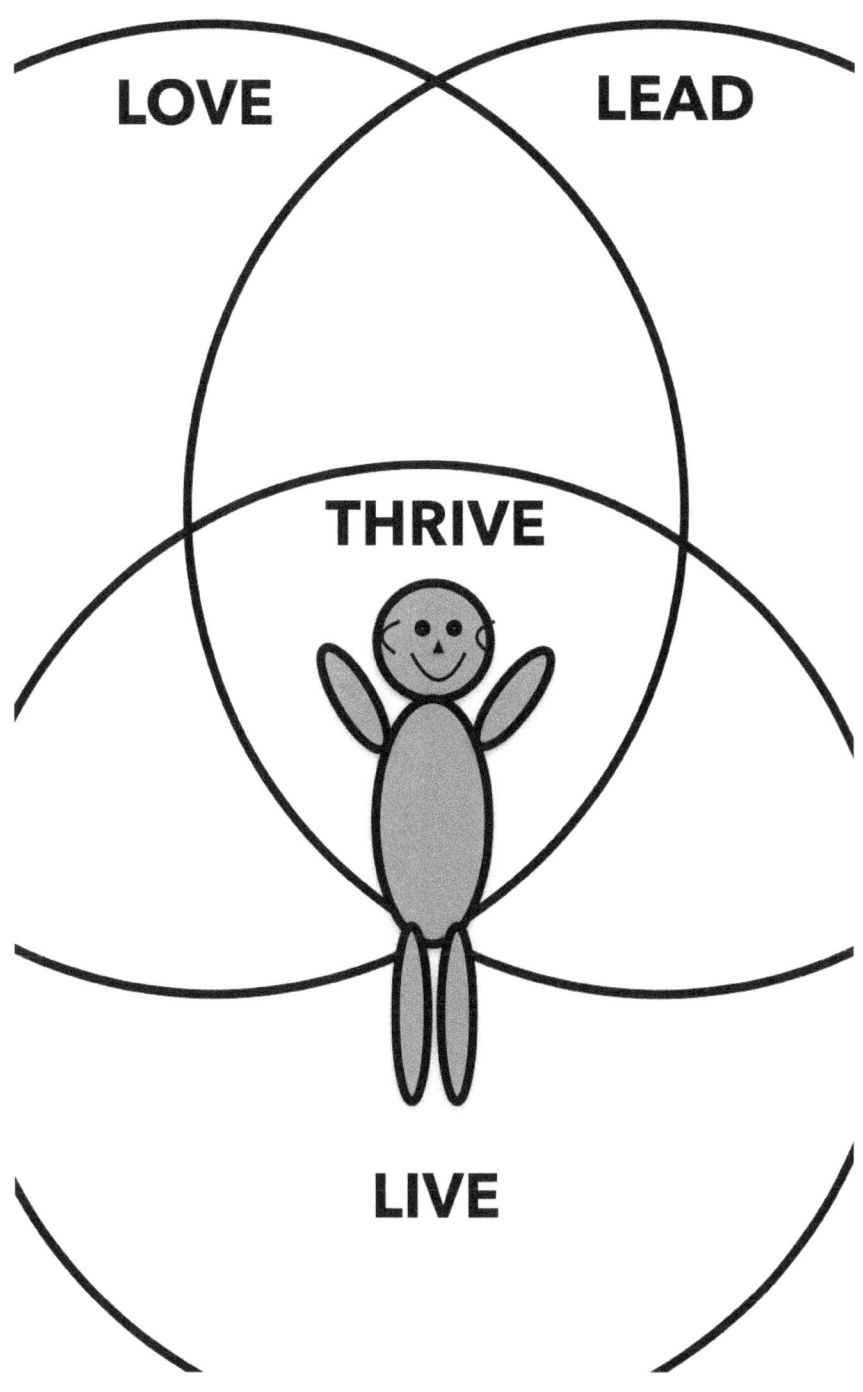

wanted to do and they were getting paid well, what would anyone have to fight about?

Yes, it's a little idealistic, but that's my dream.

Even if you don't buy into my utopian vision, I hope you see how this methodology can help you to create your own little career paradise.

Love.

Lead.

Live.

Take charge of your career.

Be your own CEO.

Thrive!

ABOUT THE AUTHORS

James Lopata, co-founder of innerOvation™ LLC, is an executive, career and entrepreneurial coach and consultant. He brings over two decades of business experience—including in digital media consulting, in the music and entertainment industries, on Wall Street, owning and operating two businesses, and in journalism—to his work in focusing professionals and business owners on what they need to do differently to create impact. He holds degrees from Miami (Ohio) and Harvard Universities. Even with all that, not much gets him more excited than Zen meditation practice.

Brenda Loan Baker, co-founder of innerOvation™ LLC, is an executive, career, and small business coach, specializing in helping women reach their highest potential. She has over two decades of corporate experience in sales and finance. Brenda loves any chance to Irish step dance.

Together, James and Brenda have been enhancing the work lives of countless professional in sharing the LOVE LEAD LIVE career development model in talks, classes, seminars, and one-on-one coaching. They are thrilled to finally be able reach a wider audience, helping as many people as possible to achieve sustainable career happiness! Yay!

www.ingramcontent.com/pod-product-compliance
Lightning Source LLC
Chambersburg PA
CBHW070334190526
45169CB00005B/1892